OUR SOLAR SYSTEM
VENUS
THE BRIGHTEST PLANET

by Mari Schuh

pogo

Ideas for Parents and Teachers

Pogo Books let children practice reading informational text while introducing them to nonfiction features such as headings, labels, sidebars, maps, and diagrams, as well as a table of contents, glossary, and index.

Carefully leveled text with a strong photo match offers early fluent readers the support they need to succeed.

Before Reading

- "Walk" through the book and point out the various nonfiction features. Ask the student what purpose each feature serves.
- Look at the glossary together. Read and discuss the words.

Read the Book

- Have the child read the book independently.
- Invite him or her to list questions that arise from reading.

After Reading

- Discuss the child's questions. Talk about how he or she might find answers to those questions.
- Prompt the child to think more. Ask: Venus has a thick, heavy atmosphere. How does this affect its temperature?

Pogo Books are published by Jump!
5357 Penn Avenue South
Minneapolis, MN 55419
www.jumplibrary.com

Library of Congress Cataloging-in-Publication Data

Names: Schuh, Mari C., 1975– author.
Title: Venus : the brightest planet / by Mari Schuh.
Description: Minneapolis, MN: Jump!, Inc., [2023]
Series: Our solar system | Includes index.
Audience: Ages 7–10
Identifiers: LCCN 2022031800 (print)
LCCN 2022031801 (ebook)
ISBN 9798885243766 (hardcover)
ISBN 9798885243773 (paperback)
ISBN 9798885243780 (ebook)
Subjects: LCSH: Venus (Planet)—Juvenile literature.
Classification: LCC QB621 .S388 2023 (print)
LCC QB621 (ebook)
DDC 523.42–dc23/eng20220919
LC record available at https://lccn.loc.gov/2022031800
LC ebook record available at https://lccn.loc.gov/2022031801

Editor: Jenna Gleisner
Designer: Emma Bersie

Photo Credits: VolodymyrSanych/Shutterstock, cover (background); Alexandr Yurtchenko/Dreamstime, cover (Venus); NASA, 1, 18–19; Dmitry Bodrov/Shutterstock, 3; Anton27/Shutterstock, 4–5; buradaki/iStock, 6–7; buradaki/Shutterstock, 8; Beyond Space/Shutterstock, 9; NASA/JPL-Caltech, 10–11 (Venus); Hermann Viria/Shutterstock, 10–11 (background); NASA/JPL, 12–13, 14–15, 16; bas/Alamy, 17; Konstantin Shaklein/Alamy, 20–21; NASA images/Shutterstock, 23.

Printed in the United States of America at Corporate Graphics in North Mankato, Minnesota.

For Paige

TABLE OF CONTENTS

Venus

Do you ever look up at the night sky? Maybe you see a lot of stars. You might see the **planet** Venus, too! It is the brightest planet in the night sky.

Venus is often called the morning star. It is also called the evening star. Why? This bright planet can be seen at sunrise and sunset.

All planets **orbit** the Sun. Venus's path is closer to Earth's than any other planet in our **solar system**.

TAKE A LOOK!

Venus is the second planet from the Sun. Take a look!

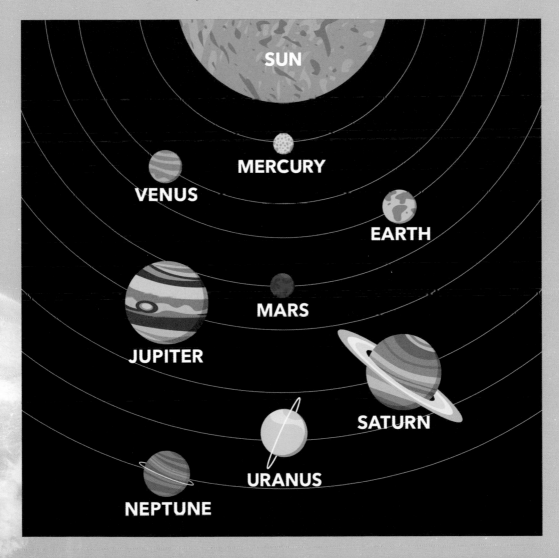

CHAPTER 2

ALL ABOUT VENUS

All planets spin. One full spin is one day. Venus spins very slowly. This means it has really long days. One spin, or day, on Venus is equal to 243 Earth days! Venus spins in the opposite direction of Earth and most other planets.

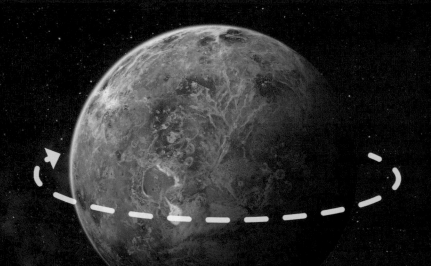

Sun

Because of this, the Sun rises in the west on Venus. The Sun sets in the east. This is opposite of what happens on Earth.

clouds

Venus is the hottest planet in the solar system. Temperatures can reach 900 degrees Fahrenheit (482 degrees Celsius). That is hot enough to melt metal!

Why is Venus so hot? It is close to the Sun. Also, its heavy **atmosphere** has layers of gases. Thick clouds always cover the planet. The gases and clouds trap heat.

DID YOU KNOW?

Clouds on Venus are made of sulfuric acid. This strong, oily acid makes the clouds smell like rotten eggs!

crater

Venus's surface is dry and rocky.
It has mountains and valleys.
Meteorites hit the planet.
They create **craters**.

TAKE A LOOK!

Venus has layers much like Earth. Take a look!

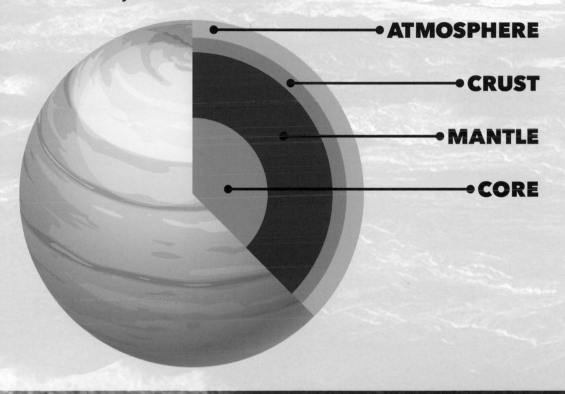

ATMOSPHERE

CRUST

MANTLE

CORE

Smooth plains are also found on Venus. **Lava** from **volcanoes** helped create these areas. Venus has thousands of volcanoes. In fact, Venus has the most volcanoes of any planet in the solar system.

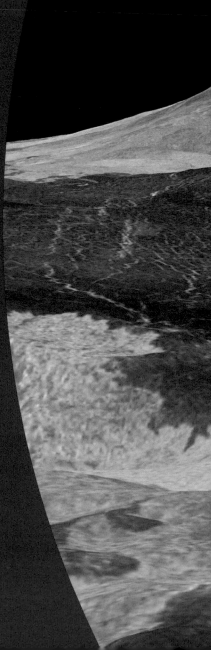

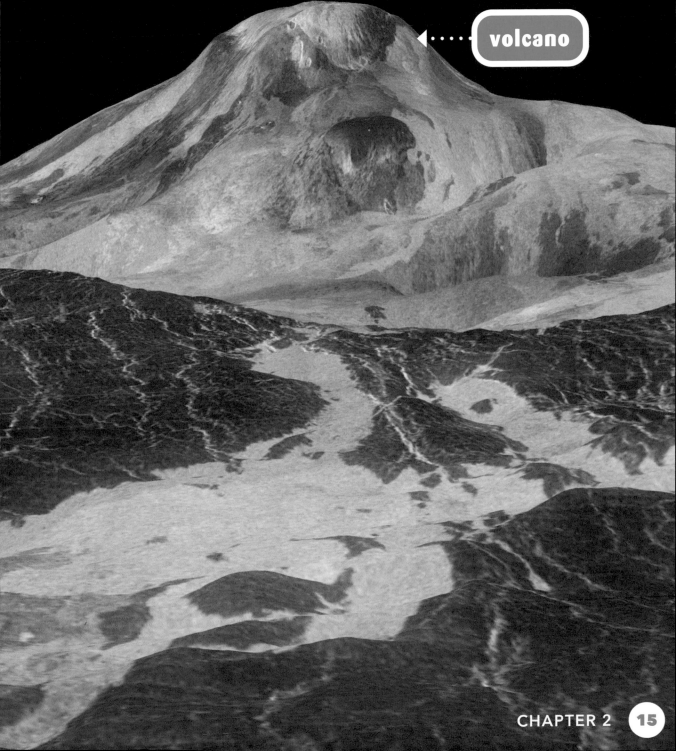

volcano

CHAPTER 3

AMAZING DISCOVERIES

In 1962, *Mariner 2* flew by Venus. It gathered information about its temperature. This made history. Why? *Mariner 2* was the first **spacecraft** to send information from another planet to Earth.

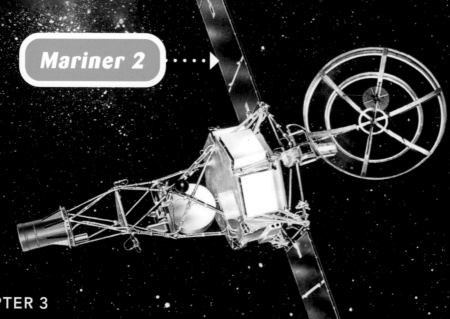

Mariner 2 ····▶

In 1970, *Venera 7* landed on Venus. It made history, too. It was the first spacecraft to land on another planet.

Venera 7 model

Magellan orbited Venus in the 1990s. It mapped almost all of the planet's surface. It took photos of Venus's tall mountains.

DID YOU KNOW?

It is hard to explore Venus's surface because it is so hot. High **pressure** makes it difficult, too. Spacecraft that land on Venus only survive one to two hours.

Magellan

Venus Express

Venus Express orbited Venus from 2006 to 2014. It found small amounts of water in the atmosphere. It also took photos of the planet's clouds.

Scientists want to learn more about Venus. What more would you like to discover about it?

DID YOU KNOW?

Venus is often called Earth's twin. Why? The planets are similar in size, **mass**, and **density**. **Gravity** on both is also about the same.

ACTIVITIES & TOOLS

TRY THIS!

TRAPPING HEAT

The heavy atmosphere and thick clouds on Venus trap heat. See how this happens with this fun activity!

What You Need:
- tall plastic bottle
- small glass jar that will fit inside the plastic bottle
- scissors
- thermometer
- paper or notebook
- pen or pencil

❶ Using the scissors, cut off the bottom of the plastic bottle. Remove the label. Keep the cap on.

❷ Put the thermometer inside the jar. Then put the jar in a sunny area.

❸ After one hour, read the temperature on the thermometer. Record the temperature.

❹ Now put the bottle over the jar.

❺ After one hour, read the temperature on the thermometer. Record the temperature.

❻ Compare the two temperatures. Which one was higher? The bottle acts like the atmosphere and clouds on Venus. It traps heat.

GLOSSARY

atmosphere: The mixture of gases that surrounds a planet.

craters: Large holes in the ground that are made when pieces of rock or metal in space crash into a planet or moon.

density: The measure of how heavy or light an object is for its size. Density is measured by dividing an object's mass by its volume.

gravity: The force that pulls things toward the center of a planet and keeps them from floating away.

lava: The hot, liquid rock that pours out of a volcano when it erupts.

mass: The amount of physical matter an object has.

meteorites: Pieces of rock or metal in space that hit a planet or moon.

orbit: To travel in a circular path around something.

planet: A large body that orbits, or travels in circles around, the Sun.

pressure: The force produced by pressing on something.

solar system: The Sun, together with its orbiting bodies, such as the planets, their moons, and asteroids, comets, and meteors.

spacecraft: Vehicles that travel in space.

volcanoes: Mountains with openings through which molten lava, ash, and hot gases can erupt.

INDEX

TO LEARN MORE

Finding more information is as easy as 1, 2, 3.

1. Go to www.factsurfer.com
2. Enter "Venus" into the search box.
3. Choose your book to see a list of websites.

FACT SURFER